A Year in the Kitchen with *Kate Lamont*

Thanks

Proudly, I thank my kitchen brigades who cook beautiful, tasty food — specifically Nathan at East Perth, Jim at Yallingup and my sister Fiona in the Swan Valley, all of whom inspire and coordinate terrific chefs within their teams. And my front of house crews, led by Voula, Jason and Matthew, who treat the businesses as if they were their own, making the restaurants a great experience every visit.

Thanks, too, to Leon Bird, who has great talent and equally great patience.

A Year in the Kitchen with *Kate Lamont*

Photographs by Leon Bird

Fremantle Arts Centre Press

Australia's finest small publisher

First published 2004 by
FREMANTLE ARTS CENTRE PRESS
25 Quarry Street, Fremantle
(PO Box 158, North Fremantle 6159)
Western Australia.
www.fremantlepress.com.au

Reprinted 2006.

Project Editor Cate Sutherland
Designer Marion Duke
Printed by Everbest Printing Co Ltd

National Library of Australia
Cataloguing-in-publication data

   Lamont, Kate, 1962- .
   A year in the kitchen with Kate Lamont.

   ISBN 1 92073 134 2.

   1. Cookery. I. Title.

   641.5

Contents

Introduction 9

Spring 11

Summer 31

Autumn 51

Winter 71

Basics 91

Kate Lamont 99

Index 100

Cooking with ingredients when they are at their best is, frankly, just common sense. There is no argument that asparagus tastes better in spring. Like new season Japanese pumpkin and the first baby peas, there is no comparison to crunching into a Fuji in June or a bunch of chilled sultanas on a hot February day, or the anticipation of sweet cherries just a week or two after they hit the market. Look, too, for freshly dried walnuts in early winter — you won't believe they can be so creamy and, well, walnutty!

When you are cooking, think through how you expect a dish to taste — robust or subtle, harmonious or in contrast — and then use individual ingredients to build those flavours. Look for new-season olive oil towards the end of autumn and taste to build a repertoire — one to drizzle, one to blend, one to offer piquancy, one to suggest richness. Similarly, explore wonderful vinegars made for their flavour as well as their acetic qualities. Don't forget butter, either. Moderation, as we know, is appropriate in all things, but you just shouldn't deprive yourself or your guests of the absolute pleasure of fresh butter. Salt and pepper, too, are often forgotten as we look to educate and extend our food horizons, yet they are possibly the best flavour enhancers of all. Season as you cook, as well as afterwards, remembering that you can always add more but can't take it out!

Seek out the deli counter or warehouse supplier — invariably some ingredients are fresher and more enticing than in the pre-packaged section at a supermarket. The fabulous blocks of Danish fetta in big briny buckets and bright pink tarama scooped from huge tubs come to mind. And nothing beats having a thick piece of rump sliced or a lamb rack trimmed in front of your very eyes.

Each season definitely has its strengths. The recipes and ideas listed in the inspirations that follow are for you to enjoy. I've created an individual menu for each month, but obviously try things in any combination you like. And, as always, for a total dining experience — whether it be a simple salad in the garden or a celebratory dinner — hunt out wines that enhance your food flavours.

Welcome spring with its endless variety of fresh, tantalising flavours. Lounge in shafts of newly-warm sunshine gobbling up just-baked tarts filled with roasted peppers, smoky eggplant and caramelised onion, washed down with light-bodied reds; or spanking-fresh seared tuna with limy, handmade mayonnaise on nests of just-cut baby rocket. Feast on asparagus so tender there's no need to trim or peel it, cooked on a barbecue, drizzled with grassy olive oil and scattered with salty, silky soft fetta. Simmer baby mussels in white wine flavoured with bay leaves, then pile on warm garlic-rubbed croutons smeared with roasted tomatoes. Delight in veal chops baked with crunchy, lemony crumb and seeded mustard, or roasted apples with frothy, marsala-infused zabaglione. Savour strawberries so sweet they don't need sugar — whip mascarpone with real vanilla to serve, warm the berries in a little Cointreau or drizzle with some sweet, reduced balsamic. Bake crunchy biscotti with loads of fennel seeds and hazelnuts, dip into sweet white wine and munch to your heart's content.

Green pea soup with black peppercorn pecorino

serves 6

6 shallots

50 g butter

salt and pepper to season

6 cups chicken stock *(page 92)*

500 g shelled peas

1 small cos lettuce

200 g snow pea shoots

100 g black peppercorn pecorino

extra virgin olive oil to serve

Dice shallots very finely and sauté in butter. Season. Add stock and bring to a simmer. Add peas and cook until barely tender. Shred lettuce and trim snow pea shoots of most of their stalks. Add lettuce and shoots to soup and cook a further 5 minutes. Blitz in a food processor. Taste for seasoning. Serve hot with lashings of shaved black peppercorn pecorino and a splash of grassy olive oil.

The vibrant colour of this soup is irresistible. The lettuce and snow pea shoots add a truly spring-like pungency and freshness.

Barbecued lamb cutlets with garlic croutons

serves 6

lamb:

12 double lamb cutlets*

salt and pepper to season

⅔ cup olive oil, plus extra to rub

⅓ cup lemon juice

2½ tablespoons red wine vinegar

croutons:

1 ciabatta loaf

5 tablespoons roasted garlic *(page 94)*

salad:

10 anchovy fillets

⅔ cup chopped flatleaf parsley

1 cup shaved parmesan

6 cups baby spinach

To prepare lamb: Rub with salt, pepper and olive oil. Leave 1 hour. Cook on a barbecue to your liking. Make a vinaigrette with lemon juice, red wine vinegar and olive oil. Spoon over cooked lamb. Rest for at least 15 minutes, covered with aluminium foil. Reserve all juices.

To make croutons: Warm roasted garlic. Slice bread and grill. Spread warm toasts with garlic.

To serve: Place lamb on plates. Chop anchovies and mix with parsley, parmesan and spinach. Use lamb juices and vinaigrette to dress. Pile croutons next to warm lamb and place spinach salad on the side.

The lemon and red wine vinegar mingled with the juices from the barbecued lamb make a most delicious dressing for the spinach. The roasted garlic croutons have a real depth of flavour and add great crunch.

* Ask your butcher to prepare the cutlets as double, that is, two chops' worth of meat on each bone.

Orange spice ice-cream with tiny truffles

serves 6

truffles:

200 g dark chocolate

50 g unsalted butter

1 tablespoon port

1 tablespoon cream

1 egg yolk

ice-cream:

3 cinnamon quills

6 allspice berries

12 cloves

1 star anise

peel of 3 oranges

1 vanilla pod

3 cups cream

1 cup milk

1 cup sugar

9 egg yolks

syrup:

1 cup sugar

1 cup water

juice of 3 oranges

2 star anise

To make truffles: Melt chocolate with butter, port and cream. Stir to a smooth paste. Add egg yolk. Cool. When firm, portion mixture into balls about the size of marbles. Chill.

To make ice-cream: Mix spices with peel and vanilla seeds scraped from pod. Heat cream and milk. Add spices and steep overnight. Strain and reheat. Mix sugar and egg yolks well. Pour the near boiling cream over the eggs and whisk. Return to heat and cook gently until thickened. Strain and cool. Churn cooled cream mixture in an ice-cream maker (or, without a maker, cool until nearly frozen then beat with an electric beater). Add truffles and mix gently. Freeze.

To make syrup: Simmer sugar, water, juice and star anise until reduced by two-thirds. Strain and cool.

To serve: Scoop ice-cream into bowls and drizzle with syrup.

Leftover truffles can be dusted with Dutch cocoa and served with coffee, or on the side of the ice-cream.

Braised duck and roasted hazelnut salad

serves 6

6 braised duck marylands (*page 80*)

4 cups rocket leaves

1 red onion, sliced finely

100 g hazelnuts

2 pears, sliced finely

1 tablespoon red wine vinegar

½ cup olive oil

salt and pepper to season

Preheat oven to 180°C. Roast hazelnuts until browned, about 10 minutes. While still hot, place nuts in a clean tea towel and rub to remove skins. Discard skins and chop nuts roughly. Warm duck in oven, 5 to 8 minutes. Remove skin and bones and shred meat into bite-sized pieces. Mix vinegar, olive oil, salt and pepper to make dressing. Gently mix all ingredients together and serve.

For maximum flavour impact it is important to mix the warm duck meat into the salad — the natural richness of the meat is enhanced by the crunchy pear and red wine vinaigrette.

Pancetta-wrapped salmon with spiced eggplant

serves 6

spiced eggplant:

3 medium eggplants

salt

olive oil to cook

6 shallots

3 cloves garlic

½ tablespoon smoky paprika

1 tablespoon turmeric

1 tablespoon ground cumin

2 tablespoons red mustard seeds

salt and pepper to season

½ cup sugar

1 cup red wine vinegar

salmon:

6 x 180 g salmon pieces

18 thin slices smoked pancetta

pepper to season

olive oil to cook

To make spiced eggplant: Preheat oven to 180°C. Cut eggplants in half lengthways. Salt, leave for 20 minutes, then wash and dry. Rub the cut sides with olive oil and roast until soft. When cool, scoop out flesh and mash to a chunky puree. You may like to remove any long lines of seeds at this stage. Sauté shallots and garlic in olive oil until translucent. Add spices and cook until aromatic. Season. Add sugar and vinegar and reduce by two-thirds. Stir constantly — as the mixture reduces it has a tendency to burn. Add eggplant and cook further until the liquid has all but disappeared and mixture is a moist paste.

To cook salmon: Wrap each piece of salmon with 3 slices of pancetta. Pan-fry with a little olive oil seasoned with pepper.

To serve: Top salmon with a dollop of warm spiced eggplant. Serve with blanched asparagus.

When serving salmon with this eggplant, the fish seems to call out to be enjoyed with a glass or two of fruity red — perfect for a sunny Sunday afternoon.

Strawberry jelly with mascarpone and shortbread crumb

serves 6

jelly:

2 cups sugar

4 cups water

500 g strawberries, hulled

8 leaves gelatine

shortbread crumb:

1 cup almond meal

1½ cups sugar

2½ cups flour

180 g melted butter

to serve:

200 g mascarpone

6 tablespoons cognac

To make jelly: Simmer water and sugar until sugar is dissolved. Remove from heat and add strawberries. Leave to steep for at least 2 hours. Drain liquid from strawberries. Reheat liquid. Soak gelatine in cold water until soft. Whisk into warmed strawberry liquid and cool. Pour into glasses, half full. Chill until set, keeping remaining liquid at room temperature. Slice half the strawberries and place on top of the set jelly. Add enough liquid to just cover. Chill until set. Top up with remaining jelly. Chill until set.

To make crumb: Preheat oven to 160°C. Combine almond meal, sugar and flour. Mix in butter to form crumble. Bake until crunchy and pale gold in colour, about 20 minutes.

To serve: Bring mascarpone to room temperature and mix with shortbread crumb. Place a dollop on the top of each jelly glass. Spoon over cognac and serve with remaining strawberries and extra crumb.

Leaving the strawberries to steep overnight allows the liquid to draw more colour from the berries, giving a vibrant pinky-red hue to the jelly. If you don't have time to set the jelly in three stages, simply fill each glass and set, then serve the strawberries on top.

October

Muneki's caviar pasta

serves 6

500 g angel hair pasta

pasta sauce:
1 brown onion, very finely sliced
3 cloves garlic, minced
5 shiitake mushrooms, sliced
500 g button mushrooms, sliced
2½ tablespoons olive oil
1½ cups sake
1 cup mirin
1½ tablespoons soy sauce
1 cup cream
sea salt and pepper

caviar mix:
2 tablespoons black Tobico
2 tablespoons yellow Tobico
4 tablespoons orange Masago
2 tablespoons green Tobico

to serve:
2 shallots, finely sliced
shaved parmesan

Cook angel hair pasta, drain and keep warm.

To make sauce: Sauté onion and garlic in olive oil until golden and aromatic. Add mushrooms. Cook. Season. Add sake, mirin and soy and reduce by half. Add cream and further reduce by half.

To serve: Mix caviars together gently. Combine hot sauce with warm pasta and caviars. Season and serve with a small amount of shaved parmesan and shallots.

I first ate this pasta at my local Japanese restaurant, Nine. While you will need to try Muneki's for the authentic experience, I think my version, which is a little simpler, is pretty tasty! The recipe uses flying fish roe which can be purchased from specialist fish suppliers.

Snapper and saffron broth

serve 6

3 leeks

3 sticks celery

6 cloves garlic

½ cup olive oil

1 teaspoon saffron threads

2 cups white wine

salt and pepper to season

8 cups fish stock *(page 93)*

6 ripe tomatoes, skinned, seeded and diced

⅓ cup arborio rice

500 g snapper

1 cup fresh mint leaves

Finely chop leeks, celery and garlic. Sauté in olive oil, taking care to keep heat low so they cook, but do not colour. Add saffron and cook a further 5 minutes. Turn heat to high to reduce any liquid and then deglaze with white wine. Season. Add stock and simmer for 10 minutes. Add tomatoes and rice. Once rice is nearly cooked, cut fish into small bite-sized pieces and add. Lower heat to allow fish to gently cook in the soup. Taste for seasoning. Add mint leaves and serve.

This is a beautiful, light main course. The rice is hardly there at all and the garlic, saffron and tomato make the broth both fragrant and tempting.

Coconut and lime cakes with caramelised mango

makes 16 small cakes

coconut and lime cakes:

1 cup almond meal

1½ cups desiccated coconut

1 cup icing sugar

1 cup caster sugar

1 cup flour

2 teaspoons baking powder

250 g unsalted butter, melted

zest of 3 limes

10 egg whites

caramelised mango:

2 mangoes

½ cup sugar

to serve:

Greek yoghurt

To make cakes: Preheat oven to 160ºC. Mix dry ingredients together. Add melted butter. Lightly whisk egg whites and lime zest to soft peaks. Fold together. Pour into greased muffin or friand tins. Bake until starting to colour and set, about 25 minutes. Cool.

To make caramelised mango: Slice mango flesh into long slivers. Toss mango in sugar and warm in a non-stick pan until sugar begins to brown.

To serve: Pile warm mango onto coconut cakes with a dollop of Greek yoghurt.

Another great way to serve these cakes is to cut out the centres and fill them with lime curd, or to make one large cake and scatter it with strawberries before baking.

Celebrate the intensity of summer with raspberries and apricots, fruit mince pies and turkey; soothing frappés and chilled oysters; champagne and crisp parmesan wafers; rare beef and horseradish layered with truly ripe tomatoes and sea salt, crammed into grainy, thick-cut bread. Pack loads of fresh mint with cool prawns and slices of chilli in damp rice paper and ice up for the beach. Barbecue ripe pineapple slices and serve with scoops of freshly-churned yoghurty ice-cream drizzled with butterscotch sauce. Slip just-picked crab meat into your mouth with a dash of pepper and squeeze of lemon. Sauté chunks of green crayfish in the shell in sizzling butter with garlic, pepper and a generous slurp of brandy. Make rosemary brushes to baste pork chops, then eat them with warm potato salad, soft egg salsa and fried capers. Freeze seedless grapes, and make blocks of frozen nectarine slices to hand to hot children home from hectic holiday adventures. Pluck backyard vine leaves to make dolmades filled with lamb mince, soft rice and pistachios. Prepare gravlax and pile onto shredded, barely cooked potato, grilled with dill and lemon. Make mountains of pesto with toasted walnuts and fresh basil and use it instead of butter on sourdough toast piled with thinly sliced coppa and warm bocconcini.

Crisp fried marron with cumin salt

serves 6

3 teaspoons sea salt

3 teaspoons pepper

3 teaspoons ground cumin

18 small marron

oil to fry

to serve:

lime wedges

crusty bread

Mix salt, pepper and cumin. Dry-fry in a pan over medium heat until quite aromatic. Cut marron in half lengthways and clean. Dust with cumin salt. Deep-fry at 170°C until crisp. Serve immediately with limes and crusty bread.

This is a simple and delicious way to prepare shellfish — yabbies or prawns can be substituted for the marron. Definitely a dish for a casual celebration, it's best eaten in your fingers but be sure to have a nutcracker for extracting the succulent meat from the claws.

Roast turkey salad with raisin tapenade

serves 6, or more as part of a buffet

turkey:

1 tablespoon Szechwan peppercorns

6 juniper berries

6 sprigs thyme

2 teaspoons salt

½ turkey breast

butter to cook

raisin tapenade:

100 g seeded raisins

100 g pitted Kalamata olives

1 teaspoon anchovy (optional)

1 tablespoon flatleaf parsley leaves

1 clove garlic

3–4 tablespoons extra virgin olive oil

ground black pepper to season

salad:

200 g Danish fetta

6 cups baby spinach

2 oranges, segmented

12 preserved artichokes, sliced

To cook turkey: Preheat oven to 180°C. Crush peppercorns with juniper and mix with thyme and salt. Rub into turkey flesh, under and over the skin. Leave to marinate for a couple of hours. Fry turkey in a pan, or on a grill plate with butter, to seal the skin. Roast for 40 minutes to 1 hour, depending on size. Cool and slice thinly.

To make tapenade: Soak raisins in hot water for 10 minutes to soften. Strain. Place all ingredients in a food processor and pulse until coarsely ground. Season with pepper to taste. Alternatively, you can hand chop the ingredients then stir through the olive oil.

To serve: Trim long stalks from spinach. Crumble fetta and mix with spinach. Toss sliced turkey with tapenade and mix with spinach, orange and artichokes.

This is a marvellous way to enjoy turkey on a hot Christmas day. The Danish fetta is both creamy and salty, and the raisins in the tapenade add sweetness to the salad.

Apricot daquoise

serves 8

daquoise:

100 g almonds

4 egg whites

1 cup caster sugar

apricot sauce:

1 kg fresh ripe apricots

1 cup sugar

1 cup water

2 strips lemon zest

to serve:

2 cups thickened cream

To make daquoise: Preheat oven to 140°C. Blanche almonds, then toast until golden. Blitz to a fine crumb. Whisk egg whites until soft peaks form. Gradually add sugar until mixture is glossy and firm. Fold in almonds. Divide mixture in half and spread onto a paper-lined baking tray to form two rounds, approximately 20 cm in diameter. Bake until the meringue is quite dry and peels away from the baking paper, about 1 hour.

To make sauce: Halve apricots and remove stones. Simmer gently with sugar and water until they disintegrate. Cool and blitz — you may like to leave small chunks of fruit in the sauce.

To serve: Spread daquoise rounds with cream and apricot sauce and stack — they will become quite fragile once laden with cream and apricots. Cut generous slices and serve with a little extra sauce if desired.

A textural jumble of crunchy meringue, sleek, smooth cream, and unctuous apricots, this dessert is irresistible — even when you're already full!

Beef tartare

makes 24 toasts

250 g lean beef eye fillet

4 tablespoons robust olive oil

pepper to season

½ cup picked flatleaf parsley leaves

¼ cup fresh thyme leaves

½ cup fresh mint leaves

¼ cup fresh basil leaves

1 tablespoon capers

1 shallot

2 anchovies and 1 tablespoon of oil from
  the anchovies

to serve:
crunchy toasts *(page 95)*

Finely dice beef. Mix thoroughly in olive oil and season with pepper. Finely chop herbs with capers, shallot, anchovies and anchovy oil. Mix herbs with beef and serve on crunchy toasts.

Just when you thought you couldn't handle any more finger food or champagne after the festivities of Christmas, you won't be able to resist these. The fresh herbs and capers are punchy and the meat becomes quite velvety when diced finely.

Barbecued prawns with oven-dried cherry tomato salsa

serves 6

prawns:

3 shallots

5 cloves garlic

3 mashed anchovies

2 tablespoons olive oil

36 green prawns, shelled
   and deveined, tails intact

salsa:

1 cup pitted Kalamata olives

1 red onion

2 roasted red capsicums *(page 96)*

1 tablespoon capers

2 punnets cherry tomatoes, oven-dried
   (page 96)

To prepare prawns: Blitz shallots, garlic, oil and anchovy to form a chunky paste. Marinate prawns in paste for at least 1 hour, then barbecue or pan-fry.

To make salsa: Chop olives, onion and capsicums. Bruise capers with the flat blade of a knife and mix with tomatoes and other ingredients. Moisten with olive oil and season.

To serve: Toss warm prawns in salsa and serve with crusty bread and salad greens.

For me, these are the flavours of summer.
The cherry tomatoes are quick to do and their
flavour is intense and very more-ish.

White chocolate slice with poached blueberries

makes 10 portions

base:

180 g butter, softened

1 cup sugar

2½ cups flour

1 teaspoon baking powder

1 teaspoon vanilla essence

2 tablespoons sweet muscat wine

filling:

200 g white chocolate

½ cup cream

750 g cream cheese

1 cup icing sugar

4 eggs

to serve:

2 punnets blueberries

3 tablespoons brown sugar

cream

To make base: Preheat oven to 150°C. Cream butter and sugar. Fold in flour and baking powder with vanilla and muscat to form a dough. Press dough into a lined tin, 30 cm x 20 cm. Bake until golden, about 20 minutes.

To make filling: Preheat oven to 160°C. Heat cream and stir in chocolate to melt. Whip cream cheese with icing sugar. Add eggs, one at a time. Fold in chocolate cream. Pour over cooked biscuit base. Bake until set, about 30 minutes.

To serve: Place berries and sugar in a pan and gently heat. The berries will soften and create their own syrup. Portion slice onto plates. Pile berries and syrup on top. Serve with cream.

You can cut tiny squares of this slice to serve with coffee. The biscuity base is a wonderful contrast to the silky filling.

Crab salad with parmesan wafers

serves 6

parmesan wafers:
150 g parmesan, grated

crab salad:
juice of 2 limes
2 cups crème fraîche
salt and pepper to season
500 g cooked crabmeat
6 medium, ripe tomatoes
2 tablespoons chopped dill
2 cups baby spinach

to serve:
fruity olive oil

To make wafers: Preheat oven to 180°C. On a lined baking sheet, make 12 parmesan circles, each about 6 cm in diameter. Bake for 8 to 10 minutes. Cool on tray. Remove carefully — they are fairly fragile — and store in an airtight container.

To make crab salad: Skin, seed and dice tomatoes. Trim stalks from spinach leaves. Mix lime juice and crème fraîche. Season and fold in crab, tomato, spinach and dill.

To serve: Sandwich crab salad between wafers. Drizzle with olive oil

It is critical to use freshly grated parmesan to make these wafers. The flavour adds a subtle bite to the creamy, limy crab salad.

Roasted coral trout with dill beurre blanc

serves 6

coral trout:

1 coral trout, about 1.3 kg

2 lemons, sliced thinly

salt and pepper to season

olive oil to cook

dill beurre blanc:

2 cups white wine

juices from cooked fish

1 cup cream

lemon juice

300 g butter

3 tablespoons fresh dill, chopped

To cook trout: Preheat oven to 180°C. Make four or five slashes through to the bone down each side of fish. Push a slice of lemon into each slash and the remainder into the cavity. Drizzle fish with olive oil and season well with salt and pepper. Wrap in aluminium foil and roast for 50 minutes. Carefully drain juices from fish, strain and reserve for beurre blanc. Rewrap fish to keep warm.

To make beurre blanc: Reduce white wine by two-thirds. Add cream and reserved fish juices and reduce to about half a cup of thick sauce. Chop butter into small pieces. Add gradually to the reduced sauce over a low heat, whisking constantly. Do not boil. Once all the butter is absorbed, add lemon juice to taste, dill and freshly ground pepper.

To serve: Portion fish onto plates and serve with beurre blanc, crispy potatoes and roasted tomatoes.

This is an incredibly easy way to cook fish and, by using the cooking juices in the sauce, it becomes deliciously sophisticated.

Roast peaches with yoghurt ice-cream and pistachio praline

serves 6

roast peaches:
⅔ cup butter, melted
½ cup sugar
6 ripe peaches

yoghurt ice-cream:
3 cups plain yoghurt, thickened
    (page 96)
2 cups cream
1 cup milk
7 egg yolks
1 cup sugar

pistachio praline:
1 cup sugar
1 cup water
½ cup shelled pistachios

To roast peaches: Preheat oven to 180°C. Mix butter and sugar. Roll peaches in mix and place on a baking tray. Dot peaches with any remaining mix and roast for 40 minutes, basting with the syrup which is formed. Cool.

To make ice-cream: Heat milk and cream. Mix egg yolks with sugar. Add hot cream and whisk. Return to heat and cook gently until thickened. Cool and blend with yoghurt. Churn in an ice-cream maker (or, without a maker, cool until nearly frozen then beat with an electric beater). Freeze.

To make praline: Gently heat sugar and water until sugar is dissolved. Simmer until caramel is formed. When quite brown, add pistachios and turn out onto a lined baking sheet. Cool then blitz, to create a combination of small pieces and nearly powdered praline.

To serve: Cut peaches in half and remove stones. Grill or pan-fry peaches to caramelise the cut side. Serve with a scoop of ice-cream and scattering of praline.

This dessert is so appealing, make sure you do extra. The warm, caramelised peaches with the deliciously tart yet creamy ice-cream and crunchy praline are a knockout.

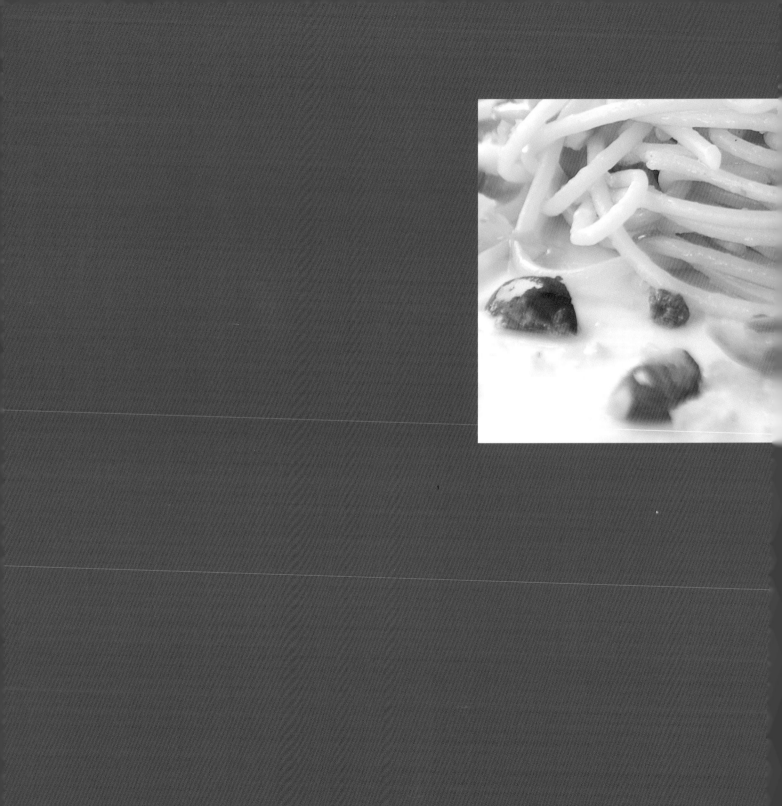

Embrace the cooler nights with aromatic curries, laden with kaffir lime and pieces of eggplant. Poach ripe, deep-burgundy plums and eat chilled for breakfast with thick yoghurt and honey toasted oats. Seek out whole baby fennel and shred to eat raw with garlicky dressing and shaved parmesan, or slice thickly and coat with egg and fresh breadcrumbs, dot with butter and bake until tender. Wrap ripe, purple figs in prosciutto, add a smear of goat cheese inside, warm through and toss with the inner leaves of new-season radicchio. Finely chop scallops and stir-fry in an instant with sweet soy and chilli, pile on fillets of roasted snapper and steamed broccolini and serve with steely, grassy sauvignon blanc and warm baguettes. Make tiny chocolate truffles rolled in Dutch cocoa and let them melt in your mouth, washed down with short espressos brimming with crema.

Lamb bites with skordalia
makes 20

lamb bites:

½ cup raw chickpeas

500 g lamb mince

½ cup mint leaves

salt and pepper to season

1 teaspoon smoky paprika

2 tablespoons butter, melted

skordalia:

2 medium potatoes

1 cup cream

salt and pepper to season

1 tablespoon roasted garlic *(page 94)*

to serve:

lemon

To make lamb bites: Soak chickpeas for at least 6 hours. Drain and blitz to a crumbly paste. Mix thoroughly with lamb mince. Chop mint leaves as finely as possible. Add to mince with salt, pepper and paprika. Form mince into balls the size of walnuts. Roll in melted butter. Cook in a pan or in the oven until browned and medium rare.

To make skordalia: Boil potatoes until well cooked. Reduce cream by half. Peel potatoes and blitz with cream, roasted garlic and seasoning. Serve warm with lamb bites and a squeeze of lemon.

Raw chickpeas add a delicious 'freshly-sprouted' taste to these meatballs. Fantastic as a snack, the lamb can also be made into larger patties and used for burgers with caramelised pumpkin and rocket, topped with skordalia.

Green olive, lemon and crunchy crumb spaghetti

serves 6

24 almonds, skin on

2 cups green olives

2 small lemons

2 tablespoons capers

2 cups fresh breadcrumbs

1 cup extra virgin olive oil

3 tablespoons lemon juice

pepper and salt to season

500 g dried spaghetti

Toast almonds until golden. Chop roughly. Pit olives and chop to the size of pine nuts. Slice lemons as finely as you can, then chop roughly. Chop capers (wash and dry first if salty). Toss breadcrumbs in a small amount of olive oil and toast until crisp and golden. Mix lemon juice with remaining oil. Season. Cook spaghetti and drain well. Combine with all the ingredients, adding the crumb last of all. Serve with cracked pepper.

The flavours in this 'sauce' are mild yet alluring. Choose plump green olives — if they're overly salty, soak them in a couple of changes of water to lessen the impact. Use robust olive oil with lots of piquancy to balance the lemon.

Toasted brazil nut cake with mascarpone

serves 8

brazil nut cake:

180 g brazil nuts

2 tablespoons semolina

6 eggs, separated

1 cup caster sugar

3 tablespoons brandy

½ cup honey

1 cup water

mascarpone:

250 g mascarpone

⅓ cup cream

3 tablespoons sugar

1 vanilla pod

To make cake: Preheat oven to 180°C. Toast nuts until golden then blitz finely. Mix nuts with semolina. Whisk egg yolks and half a cup of the sugar until thick. Fold in nuts and brandy. Whisk egg whites to firm peaks. Fold together and pour into a 22 cm tin. Cook until set, about 30 minutes. Simmer remaining sugar, honey and water together for 5 minutes to make a syrup. Pour half the hot syrup over the warm cake while still in its tin. Chill remaining syrup. Turn cake out when cool.

To make mascarpone cream: Whisk mascarpone with sugar and vanilla seeds scraped from pod. Gradually add cream until incorporated.

To serve: Cut cake into small slices and serve with the mascarpone cream and a drizzle of reserved syrup.

This cake is beautifully moist. It can also be used as a mould to frame ice-cream, or made into tiny friands sandwiched together with mascarpone.

Saffron filo tarts with scallops and snow pea salad

serves 6

saffron filo tarts:

3 sheets filo pastry

olive oil

1 teaspoon saffron

½ cup white wine

6 eggs

2 cups cream

salt and pepper to season

6 shallots

1 tablespoon butter

snow pea salad:

100 g snow peas

1 packet snow pea shoots

1 packet chervil

1 packet fennel

½ cup olive oil

¼ cup chardonnay vinegar (or similar)

18 scallops

To make tarts: Preheat oven to 170°C. Layer filo, three sheets thick, with olive oil brushed sparingly between each layer. Cut filo into squares and line oiled muffin tins. Simmer white wine with saffron for 1 minute. Cool. Mix eggs and cream. Season and add saffron wine. Finely dice shallots and sauté in butter until soft. Place shallots evenly in each lined tin and fill with egg mix. Bake until egg is set. Cool and gently remove from tins.

To make salad: Julienne snow peas. Trim snow pea shoots. Pick chervil and fennel from stalks. Mix. Moisten with vinaigrette made from olive oil and vinegar. Season.

To serve: Warm the tarts in a moderate oven. Sear scallops. Place three scallops on each tart. Add salad. Drizzle with extra vinaigrette and serve.

Filo provides a great light crunch to nurse this delicate custard, and the chervil and fennel enhance the taste of the simply cooked scallops. It is worth seeking out chardonnay vinegar, as it marries the flavours beautifully.

Rare beef salad with tarragon mayonnaise

serves 6

beef:

1 beef tenderloin (about 750 g clean weight)

olive oil

salt and pepper to season

salad:

200 g baby green beans

4 roasted red capsicums (*page 96*)

6 medium, ripe tomatoes

2 cups flatleaf parsley leaves

6 cups assorted greens (rocket, baby spinach,
   snow pea shoots)

5 slices of day-old, robust bread

olive oil to drizzle

reduced balsamic:

2 cups balsamic vinegar

1 cup port

1 tablespoon brown sugar

to serve:

1 cup aioli (*page 95*)

1 tablespoon fresh tarragon, chopped

To cook beef: Tie to retain shape. Rub with salt, pepper and olive oil. Leave to come to room temperature, then seal in a hot pan. Roast for 15 minutes in a hot oven or longer to your preference. Rest for at least 30 minutes in a warm place.

To make salad: Blanch beans in boiling, salted water until barely cooked, about 2 to 3 minutes. Cook in batches so the water doesn't come off the boil when beans are added. Refresh in cold water immediately. Drain. Slice capsicum into bite-sized pieces. Skin, seed and dice tomatoes. Remove crusts and tear bread into bite-sized pieces. Place bread on a baking tray. Drizzle with olive oil and bake until golden. Cool.

To make dressing: Simmer balsamic vinegar, port and brown sugar together until reduced to less than 1 cup of syrup. Cool.

To serve: Slice beef into a bowl to ensure you capture all the meat juices. Add salad and mix together gently. Season. Fold through aioli. Serve drizzled with reduced balsamic.

This salad makes a wonderful platter for sharing on a warm, lazy afternoon, accompanied by lots of wine and great conversation. I find I keep coming back to have just another morsel of beef, or to crunch one more bean dipped in the juicy mayo.

Hazelnut crème with espresso-poached dates

serves 6

hazelnut crème:

1 cup hazelnuts

3½ cups cream

1 vanilla pod

3 tablespoons caster sugar

9 egg yolks

2 tablespoons Frangelico

sugar to serve

espresso-poached dates:

18 dates

1 cup sugar

2½ cups strong coffee

To make crème: Roast hazelnuts. While still hot, tip nuts onto a clean tea towel and rub briskly. Discard skins. Chop nuts finely or pulse in a food processor. Heat cream with nuts and vanilla seeds scraped from pod. Steep for two hours. Strain and reheat cream. Mix sugar with yolks. Pour hot cream over yolks and mix well. Return to heat and cook gently until mixture thickens. Strain. Add Frangelico and pour into ramekins. Bake at 140°C in a water bath until set, about 40 minutes. Chill.

To poach dates: Combine sugar and coffee. Heat until sugar is dissolved. Add dates and cook gently for 20 minutes. Cool in syrup. Remove dates, peel and pit. Store in syrup.

To serve: Sprinkle tops of crèmes with sugar. Caramelise under a grill or with a hand-held burner. Slice dates into slivers. Place dates on top of crèmes and serve.

Frangelico is a digestive that infuses and lifts the creaminess of the custard. Seek out a hand-held propane burner from a hardware store; they're not hard to use and the crunchy, caramelised tops offer great texture and flavour.

Rosti with taramasalata and fried basil

serves 6

rosti:

8 medium ruby blue potatoes

salt and pepper to season

1 cup finely chopped basil

butter to cook

taramasalata:

5 thick slices robust, day-old white bread

100 g of tarama

1 clove garlic, minced

3 tablespoons lemon juice

⅔ cup fruity olive oil

pepper to season

basil:

2 cups picked basil leaves

oil to cook

To make rosti: Simmer potatoes in salted water until barely cooked (you should be able to just force the point of a knife all the way through). Drain, peel and grate into a bowl. Season with salt and pepper and add basil. Form into circles about 2 cm high and 8 cm in diameter. Chill.

To make taramasalata: Soak bread in water until softened. Squeeze out excess water and mix with tarama and garlic to a paste. Add lemon juice and drizzle in olive oil. Season with pepper.

To fry basil: Divide into three batches. Heat oil to 170°C. Cook each batch for 1 minute. Drain on absorbent paper and season with salt.

To serve. Cook rosti in butter over medium heat until golden and crisp. Portion onto plates. Spoon taramasalata on top and scatter with fried basil.

If you take the time to hunt out tarama from a shop that stocks it in bulk rather than in small tubs, you will be thrilled with the result. The salty, fishy, lemony sauce is a perfect foil to the crunchy rostis.

May

Preserved-lemon chicken with radicchio

serves 6

chicken:

12 boneless, skinless chicken thighs

2 quarters preserved lemon rind

3 tablespoons olive oil

12 sprigs thyme

pepper to season

salad:

4 slices robust bread

1 bulb garlic

½ cup olive oil, plus 4 tablespoons

2 radicchio

2 avocados

2 tablespoons sherry vinegar

salt and pepper to season

To cook chicken: Trim fat from chicken. Pound lemon rind to a paste. Add olive oil, thyme and pepper. Rub paste over chicken and leave to marinate for a couple of hours. Pan-fry chicken over medium heat. Rest in a warm place.

To make salad: Cut bread into bite-sized pieces. Smash bulb of garlic so it fragments. Heat the half cup of olive oil and fry garlic, skin and all, to flavour the oil. Remove garlic and fry bread until golden. Remove any damaged outside leaves from radicchio. Break hearts and larger leaves into smallish pieces. Slice avocados. Make a dressing with the 4 tablespoons of olive oil and the sherry vinegar. Season. Toss dressing through radicchio to coat well. Add avocado and croutons. Serve with the warm chicken.

The refreshing bitterness of the radicchio coupled with creamy avocado and moist, lemony chicken form a simple, honest and inviting combination.

Bitter chocolate cake with mandarin syrup

serves 10

bitter chocolate cake:

250 g dark bitter chocolate

200 g dark chocolate

200 g butter

9 eggs

1 cup flour

½ cup Cointreau

¾ cup sugar

mandarin syrup:

12 mandarins

1 cup sugar

2 tablespoons Cointreau

to serve:

Dutch cocoa

To make cake: Preheat oven to 180°C. Melt chocolate and butter over a bain-marie. Separate eggs. Whisk yolks until very thick. Fold in melted chocolate, then Cointreau and flour. Whisk egg whites to a soft peak. Gradually add sugar while whisking until very firm and glossy. Gently fold whites into chocolate mixture until well incorporated. Bake until barely set, about 35 minutes. Cool.

To make syrup: Juice mandarins and strain. Simmer with sugar for 10 minutes. Add Cointreau. Chill.

To serve: Allow cake to return to room temperature. Slice and dust heavily with Dutch cocoa. Place onto plates and pour syrup around cake.

Mandarin has a perfume and flavour which are very appealing with bitter chocolate. I first tried this at a friend's place for dinner. I loved it then, and I still do.

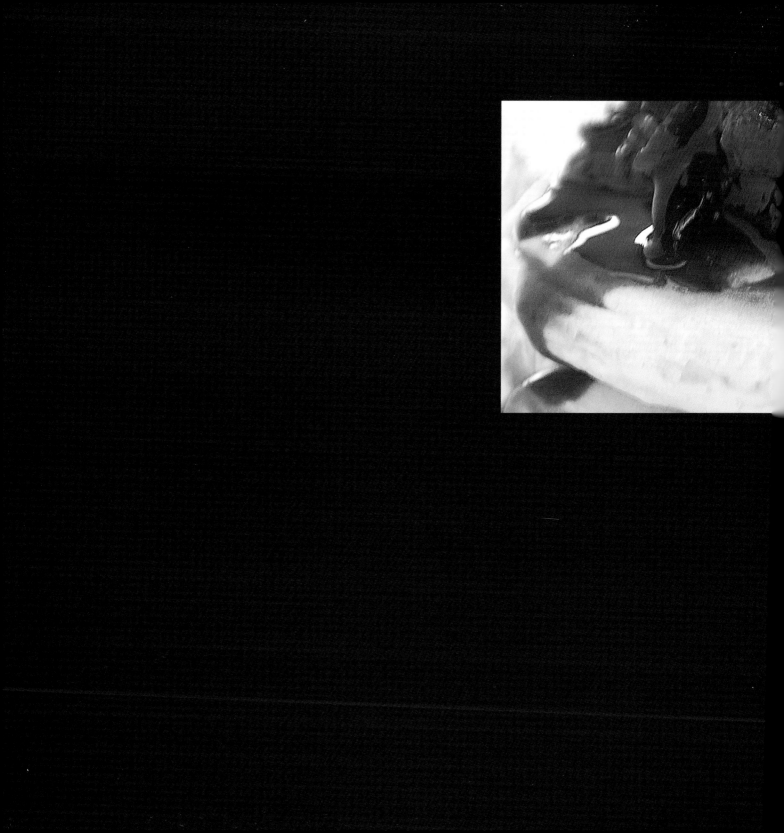

Cold hands and welcome, soaking rains demand steaming soups and tasty stews filled with pungent herbs and robust flavours served with creamy, gratineed potatoes and warm hearts. Bake crunchy-edged bread-and-butter puddings, oozing with marmalade and lashings of thick cream. Add a slurp of sherry vinegar to a chunky dhufish chowder. Liven up a quick meal of risotto with caramelised pumpkin and buttery fried sage. Roast a piece of porterhouse larded with speck, rubbed all over with cinnamon and star anise, and serve it with goat cheese and garlic-flavoured mash. Take the time to make rough puff pastry and bake flaky pithiviers loaded with savoury fillings — buttery sweated leeks, gruyere and pine nuts, spinach and ricotta, or sharp fetta and tiny sweet currants. Roll pastry over rows of anchovy and pecorino and twist into crunchy pastry sticks to munch with glasses of aged shiraz, perfect for nights of tall stories around crackling fires. Make thick strips of pappardelle and toss them with slow-cooked lamb shank eased from the bone, slivers of poached quince and braising liquid reduced to a flavoursome glaze. Poach pears in red wine, dip in yeasty batter and serve piping hot flooded with icing sugar.

Cauliflower fritters with soft egg salad

serves 6

fritters:

small cauliflower (about 500 g)

6 shallots, sliced finely

80 g butter

150 g fresh goat cheese

½ cup flour

1 tablespoon chopped chervil

1 egg

salt and pepper to season

olive oil to cook

salad:

3 eggs

2½ tablespoons sherry vinegar

½ cup olive oil

salt and pepper to season

200 g speck

1 cup flatleaf parsley

½ cup chervil

1 tablespoon capers

To make fritters: Cut cauliflower into small florets and sauté with sliced shallots in butter until golden and tender. Cool and mash gently with goat cheese, flour, chervil and egg. Season. Portion mixture into rounds about the size of a mandarin. Flatten and deep-fry in plenty of olive oil until golden, crunchy and cooked through.

To make salad: Place eggs in cold water and bring to the boil. Simmer for 2 minutes, drain and plunge into cold water. Eggs should be soft-boiled. Peel. Mix vinegar and olive oil to make a dressing. Season. Meanwhile, chop speck into small strips and fry in its own fat until crisp. Drain and discard fat. Wash excess salt from capers and dry. Mix warm speck with herbs, capers, and dressing.

To serve: Scatter salad over hot cauliflower fritters. Lay sliced egg around fritters and serve immediately.

This is a great entree for a grey winter day. Goat cheese gives the cauliflower a real liveliness and the crunchy speck and soft egg are friendly flavours.

Roast pork rack with rosemary and fennel-seed and caramelised pears

serves 6

roast pork:
6 cloves garlic
2 tablespoons fennel seeds
3 stalks rosemary
sea salt and pepper to season
olive oil
1 x 6 chop pork rack

caramelised pears:
6 beurre bosc pears
3 tablespoons brown sugar
100 g butter

crunchy potatoes:
18 small ruby blue potatoes
olive oil
sea salt and pepper to season
bay leaves

buttery spinach:
3 cloves garlic, minced
100 g butter to cook
3 bunches English spinach

To roast pork: Pound garlic, fennel seeds and rosemary together with pepper. Add a little olive oil to moisten. Trim pork of skin and fat. Smother pork flesh with the paste and marinate overnight, or for at least 6 hours. Season with sea salt and roast in a moderate oven for 45 minutes. Rest meat for 30 minutes in a warm place before serving.

To caramelise pears: Quarter and core pears. Roll in brown sugar. Sauté in butter to colour. Place on a baking tray and roast for 30 minutes, timing them to be ready just as the pork has finished resting.

To cook potatoes: Parboil. Drain and gently squash so they fragment, but still retain their shape. Toss in olive oil with sea salt, pepper and two or three bay leaves. Roast on baking tray with the pears.

To serve: In a large saucepan, fry minced garlic in butter, then add spinach and wilt. Drain away any liquid. Pile potatoes and pears onto a platter next to pork, spoon over pan juices. Add spinach and serve.

This is a sensational roast. The caramelised pears and buttery spinach give the pork a lift without gravy.

Apple galette

serves 8

1 cup walnuts

5 Granny Smith apples

2 tablespoons brown sugar

100 g butter

1 quantity rough puff pastry *(page 97)*

to serve:

vanilla ice-cream

Preheat oven to 220°C. Roast walnuts until coloured and aromatic. While still hot, tip nuts onto a clean tea towel and rub briskly. Discard skins. Chop nuts finely. Peel apples and slice into eighths. Sauté apples and brown sugar in butter until quite soft and well caramelised. Roll pastry into a circle, roughly 30 cm in diameter. Scatter nuts onto pastry, leaving a 5 cm border around the edge. Drain any liquid from apples. Carefully place apple over nuts. Fold the edges of the pastry in towards the centre. Bake until galette is golden and crunchy, about 20 minutes.

To serve: Cut galette into wedges and serve with ice-cream.

This rustic galette is at once flaky, buttery and succulent.

Sage and blue cheese frittata with shaved fennel and prosciutto

serves 6

frittata:

1 tablespoon olive oil

4 shallots, diced finely

1 tablespoon capers, washed of excess salt
   and dried

⅓ cup sage leaves, shredded

tops of two fennel bulbs

9 eggs

salt and pepper to season

200 g strongly flavoured blue cheese

salad:

2 small fennel bulbs

salt and pepper to season

3 tablespoons olive oil

1 tablespoon chardonnay vinegar

1 red onion, sliced finely

½ cup shaved parmesan

to serve:

18 thin slices prosciutto

To make frittata: Preheat oven to 170°C. In a non-stick oven pan sauté shallots, capers and sage. Finely slice fennel tops and add. Continue to cook over medium heat until soft and almost caramelised. Whisk eggs and season. Pour eggs into pan and cook for a couple of minutes, moving base of the mixture around with a fork. Add cheese in small pieces then place in oven. Bake until barely set, about 8 minutes.

To make salad: Shave fennel bulbs on a mandolin, or slice as finely as you can with a knife. Season with salt and pepper and moisten with olive oil and vinegar. Add red onion and parmesan.

To serve: Slide frittata out of pan onto a platter and serve immediately, piled with the salad and prosciutto.

When you buy the prosciutto, insist that it is freshly and very finely sliced — paper-thin prosciutto is delicious with the warm, cheesy egg.

Braised duck with polenta and orange

serves 6

braised duck:
1 tablespoon salt
12 duck marylands
1 teaspoon cloves
2 oranges, sliced thinly, peel on
3 cinnamon quills
2 carrots
1 bulb garlic
2 onions
2 sticks celery
2 cups port, reduced by half
2 cups red wine, reduced by half
4 cups chicken stock *(page 92)*

polenta:
2 cups chicken stock *(page 92)*
2 cups milk
salt and pepper to season
200 g fine polenta
2½ tablespoons cream
2 tablespoons thyme, chopped

caramelised shallots:
24 shallots
½ cup olive oil
1 tablespoon brown sugar

to serve:
brussels sprouts
julienned orange zest

To braise duck: Rub salt into duck skin. Marinate overnight with cloves, orange and cinnamon. Brush off marinade and seal duck in a pan. Chop vegetables roughly and place in baking tray. Place duck legs on top of vegetables. Add port, wine and stock. Cover with aluminium foil and braise in 180°C oven for 1 hour, or until duck is tender. Cool. Strain and reduce braising liquid by two-thirds.

To make polenta: Mix stock and milk. Heat and season. Remove from heat and add polenta in a steady stream, whisking continuously. Return to a low heat and stir continuously for 10 minutes until a smooth, creamy consistency is formed. Add cream and thyme. Set in a shallow tin. Portion when set.

To caramelise shallots: Peel and sauté in olive oil until starting to colour. Season. Add sugar and continue to cook over low heat until quite dark and softened.

To serve: Reheat duck in reduced liquid. Remove duck and further reduce liquid with orange zest to a sauce consistency. Steam brussels sprouts until tender. Drizzle with olive oil and season. Warm polenta. Portion onto plates with brussels sprouts and duck, moisten with reduced braising liquid.

Cooking duck in this way is less daunting than you might imagine. The mild, creamy polenta balances the rich and succulent meat.

Rosewater pannacotta with vanilla poached quince and pear

serves 8

rosewater pannacotta:

4 cups cream

⅔ cup caster sugar

1½ tablespoons rosewater

1 vanilla pod

5 sheets gelatine

poached fruit:

3 quince

3 beurre bosc pears

2 cups water

2 cups sugar

2 vanilla pods

To make pannacotta: Bring two-thirds of a cup of cream to the boil with sugar, vanilla pod and seeds scraped from vanilla pod. Soak gelatine in cold water until soft. Squeeze out excess water and whisk into hot cream. Add remaining cream and rosewater. Cool over ice until beginning to set, then pour into moulds and chill.

To poach fruit: Mix sugar, water and vanilla seeds scraped from pods. Heat until sugar is dissolved. Carefully peel, core and slice quince and simmer for at least 1 hour until tender and a pale pinky-orange colour. Cool in syrup. Remove quince. Peel, core and slice pears. Poach in quince syrup until tender. Cool.

To serve: Turn out pannacotta. Scatter with poached fruit and drizzle with syrup.

The scented fruit should retain a firm bite to contrast with the creamy base of smooth, perfumed pannacotta.

Citrus quail with garlicky coleslaw

serves 6

quail:

12 semi-boned quail

zest of 3 lemons

zest of 3 oranges

2 tablespoons olive oil

salt and pepper to season

coleslaw:

2 cloves garlic, minced

½ cup olive oil

1 tablespoon white wine vinegar

zest and juice of 2 lemons

zest and juice of 1 orange

salt and pepper to season

half a green cabbage

1 small red onion

1 cup watercress

To cook quail: Cut quail in half lengthways and marinate in zests with olive oil and seasoning for a couple of hours. Grill or pan-fry over medium heat.

To make coleslaw: Mix garlic, olive oil, vinegar, zest and juice to make a dressing. Season. Slice cabbage and onion as finely as possible. Remove stalks from watercress. Mix cabbage, onion, and watercress with half the dressing.

To serve: Pile coleslaw in nests onto plates. Stack quail halves on top and drizzle with remaining dressing.

It is really important to cook the quail on a medium heat so that the subtlety of the citrus is not lost. And, the finer you can slice the cabbage, the better the garlicky dressing will souse the salad.

Calamari with dhal and crisped red onions

serves 6

dhal:

2 onions, diced finely

4 cloves garlic, minced

½ cup olive oil

1 tablespoon coriander powder

1 tablespoon cumin powder

1 tablespoon paprika

½ tablespoon turmeric

250 g red lentils

2 tablespoons tomato paste

440 ml can crushed tomatoes

3 cups water

salt and pepper to season

calamari:

500 g cleaned calamari

sea salt and pepper to season

cornflour to dust

olive oil to cook

crisped red onions:

1 large or 2 medium red onions

oil to fry

To make dhal: Fry onion and garlic in olive oil. Add spices and cook until aromatic. Add lentils, cook 1 minute. Add tomato paste, tomatoes and water. Cook over medium/low heat stirring occasionally until lentils are soft, about 50 minutes. Season with salt and pepper.

To cook calamari: Score calamari if necessary, and cut into bite-sized pieces. Season well. Dust with cornflour. Cook quickly on a flat grill or non-stick pan in a little olive oil; it is best done in batches to prevent stewing.

To crisp onions: Slice onions as finely as possible. Heat oil to 170°C. Fry onion until crisp. Drain on paper. Season with salt.

To serve: Place calamari on warmed dhal and top with crisped red onions.

This recipe comes from our Margaret River kitchen. We sometimes serve the dhal and crisped onions with baby marron or fresh whiting instead of calamari. I like to leave the dhal with some texture, rather than making it too smooth.

Buttermilk pancakes and rhubarb

serves 6

rhubarb:
2 kg rhubarb
1 cup sugar

pancakes:
3 cups self-raising flour
¼ cup sugar
4 eggs
2½ cups buttermilk
2 vanilla pods

To poach rhubarb: Trim rhubarb and cut into 5 cm pieces. Place in a pan with sugar and cook over low heat until rhubarb is tender.

To make pancakes: Mix flour, sugar and vanilla seeds scraped from pods. Make a well in the centre. Mix eggs with buttermilk. Whisk into dry ingredients to make a smooth batter. Rest batter for 30 minutes. Ladle a scant half-cup of batter onto a non-stick pan. As the top of the pancake begins to bubble, flip over and colour the other side. Place pancakes in a stack and keep warm in a low oven until all are cooked. You should get roughly 18 pancakes. Serve with warmed rhubarb and cream.

These pancakes are absolute winter favourites — for adults and children alike! They are deceptively light, yet can handle chunky rhubarb, or even bacon and maple syrup for a super-indulgent breakfast.

Basics

Chicken stock

3 chicken carcasses

2 carrots

1 celery stick

1 brown onion

1 bulb garlic

¼ cup olive oil

1 cup white wine

6 peppercorns

10 parsley stalks

6 fresh thyme stalks

Preheat oven to 140°C. Roughly chop vegetables. Roast carcasses and vegetables in a baking tray with olive oil until browned. Tip into stockpot. Place the baking tray on top of stove and add wine. Reduce the wine by half over medium heat. Scrape any meat and vegetables from the bottom of the baking tray and add them and the reduced wine to stockpot with herbs and peppercorns. Cover with cold water and bring to boil. Skim regularly. At boiling point turn heat down and simmer for 2–3 hours. Strain, discard vegetables and carcasses. Cool.

Keeps for 2–3 days in the fridge, or frozen for up to a month.

Fish stock

2 fish heads

2 carrots

1 celery stick

1 brown onion

1 bulb garlic

¼ cup olive oil

2 fish carcasses

6 parsley stalks

6 peppercorns

slice lemon rind

1 cup white wine

Remove the eyes and gills from the heads. Roughly chop vegetables. In a large stockpot sauté vegetables in oil for 10 minutes over low heat. Add fish heads and carcasses, parsley stalks, peppercorns and lemon rind and turn heat to high. Add white wine and reduce for a couple of minutes. Cover with cold water and bring to the boil. Skim regularly. At boiling point, turn heat down and simmer gently for 30 minutes. Strain, discard vegetables and fish. Cool.

Keeps for 2–3 days in the fridge, or frozen for up to a month.

Mayonnaise

makes 1½ cups

1 egg yolk
½ teaspoon salt
½ teaspoon pepper
2 tablespoons lemon juice
⅔ cup fruity olive oil
½ cup mild olive oil or vegetable oil

By hand or in a food processor whisk yolk with seasoning and lemon juice. Gradually drizzle in the oils, whisking continuously until oil is incorporated. Taste — you may need more salt. This recipe can also be used as a base for any flavoured mayonnaise.

If you take the time to make mayonnaise by hand, you will enjoy a much thicker, more velvety consistency.

Roasted garlic

makes 2 tablespoons

2 bulbs garlic
1 tablespoon olive oil
salt and pepper to season
3 sprigs fresh thyme

Preheat oven to 180°C. Place unpeeled garlic and thyme in aluminium foil. Drizzle with olive oil and wrap. Roast until very soft, about 40 minutes. Be extremely careful as the roasted garlic will retain its heat for a long time. When cool, squeeze garlic pulp from the skins.

Aioli

makes 1½ cups

2 tablespoons roasted garlic
1 teaspoon Dijon mustard
1½ cups mayonnaise

Fold garlic and mustard into mayonnaise.

Crunchy toasts

makes about 36 pieces

1 baguette
salt and pepper to season
olive oil to drizzle

Preheat oven to 180°C. Slice bread as thinly as you can. Place slices in a single layer on a baking tray. Season generously with sea salt and freshly ground pepper and drizzle with olive oil. Bake until golden, about 10 minutes. Cool and store in an airtight container for up to 2 weeks.

Index

aioli   95

apple galette   76

apricot daquoise   36

apricot sauce   36

barbecued lamb cutlets   14

barbecued prawns   40

basil, fried   64

beef salad   60

beef tartare   38

beurre blanc, dill   46

bitter chocolate cake   68

blueberries, poached   42

blue cheese frittata   78

braised duck   80

braised duck salad   18

brazil nut cake   56

broth, snapper and saffron   26

buttermilk pancakes   88

cake, bitter chocolate   68

cake, toasted brazil nut   56

cakes, coconut and lime   28

calamari   86

capsicum, roasted red   96

caramelised mango   28

caramelised pears   74

caramelised shallots   80

cauliflower fritters   72

caviar pasta, Muneki's   24

cherry tomato salsa   40

chicken stock   92

chicken, preserved-lemon   66

chocolate, white slice   42

chocolate cake   68

citrus quail   84

coconut and lime cakes   28

coleslaw, garlicky   84

coral trout, roasted   46

crab salad   44

crisp fried marron   32

crisped red onions   86

croutons, garlic   14

crunchy toasts   95

dhal   86

daquoise, apricot   36

dates, espresso-poached   62

dill beurre blanc   46

duck, braised   80

duck, braised and roasted hazelnut salad   18

egg salad   72

eggplant, spiced   20

espresso-poached dates   62

fennel salad   78

filo tarts with scallops   58

fish stock   93

fried basil   64

frittata, sage and blue cheese   78
fritters, cauliflower   72

galette, apple   76
garlic croutons   14
garlic, roasted   94
garlicky coleslaw   84
green pea soup   12

hazelnut crème   62

ice-cream, orange spice   16
ice-cream, yoghurt   48

jelly, strawberry   22

lamb bites   52
lamb cutlets, barbecued   14

mandarin syrup   68
mango, caramelised   28
marron, crisp fried   32
mayonnaise   94
mayonnaise, tarragon   60
Muneki's caviar pasta   24

olive, lemon and crunchy crumb spaghetti   54
onions, crisped red   86
orange spice ice-cream   16
oven-dried cherry tomatoes   96

pancakes, buttermilk   88
pancetta-wrapped salmon   20
pannacotta, rosewater   82
parmesan wafers   44
pasta, Muneki's caviar   24
pastry, quick rough puff   97
pea soup   12
peaches, roast   48
pear, poached   82
pears, caramelised   74
pistachio praline   48
poached blueberries   42
poached dates   62
poached pear   82
poached quince   82
poached rhubarb   88
polenta   80
pork rack, roast   74
potato rosti   64
potatoes, crunchy   74
praline, pistachio   48
prawns, barbecued   40
preserved-lemon chicken   66

quail, citrus   84
quick rough puff pastry   97
quince, poached   82

radicchio salad   66
raisin tapenade   34

rare beef salad   60
red capsicum, roasted   96
red onions, crisped   86
rhubarb, poached   88
roast peaches   48
roast pork rack   74
roast turkey salad   34
roasted coral trout   46
roasted garlic   94
roasted red capsicum   96
rosewater pannacotta   82
rosti, potato   64
rough puff pastry   97

saffron filo tarts with scallops   58
sage and blue cheese frittata   78
salad, braised duck and roasted hazelnut   18
salad, crab   44
salad, fennel   78
salad, radicchio   66
salad, rare beef   60
salad, roast turkey   34
salad, snow pea   58
salad, soft egg   72
salmon, pancetta-wrapped   20
scallops   58
shallots, caramelised   80
shortbead crumb   22
skordalia   52
slice, white chocolate   42

snapper and saffron broth   26
snow pea salad   58
soup, green pea   12
spaghetti, olive, lemon and crunchy crumb   54
spiced eggplant   20
spinach, buttery   74
stock, chicken   92
stock, fish   93
strawberry jelly   22
syrup, mandarin   68

tapenade, raisin   34
taramasalata   64
tarragon mayonnaise   60
tartare, beef   38
thickened yoghurt   96
toasted brazil nut cake   56
toasts, crunchy   95
tomato, oven-dried cherry   96
truffles   16
turkey salad   34

vanilla poached quince and pear   82

white chocolate slice   42

yoghurt ice-cream   48
yoghurt, thickened   96